This Little
Hand

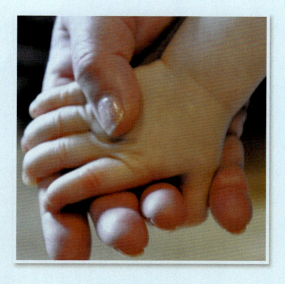

Nelda R. Symonds

Published by Tania Symonds

To order additional copies of this book, contact:
Xlibris
1-888-795-4274
www.Xlibris.com
Orders@Xlibris.com

ISBN: Softcover   978-1-7960-6554-1
        EBook   978-1-7960-6553-4

Print information available on the last page

Rev. date: 10/10/2019

This book is dedicated to our mother
Nelda R Symonds.
A loving mother, Grandmother & Great-Grandmother
Nelda enjoyed writing poems and wrote this one for us (her Daughters) when we were very young. This is one of our favorites and we feel fortunate to be able to share this book with past, present and future generations of children everywhere.

This Little Hand

This Little Hand

So Tiny and Small

This Little Hand

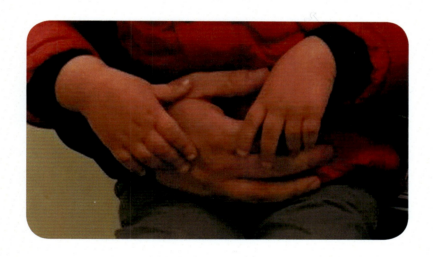

That's hardly at all

This little hand

Will laugh and grow

This little hand

may play in dough

This little hand

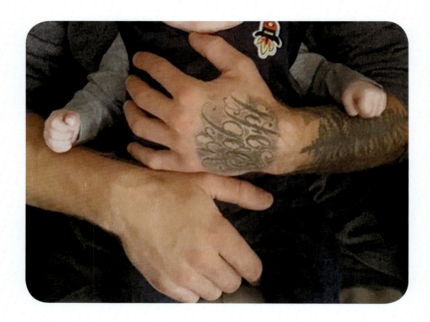

Will know strength in time

This little hand

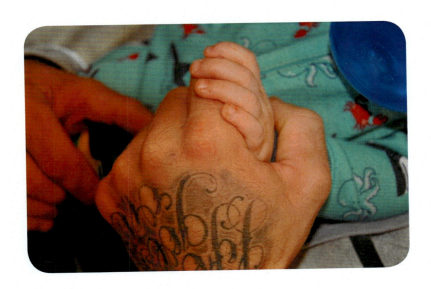

That's so like mine

This little hand

FIRST DAY
OF
1ST GRADE
2019

Will want to learn

This little hand

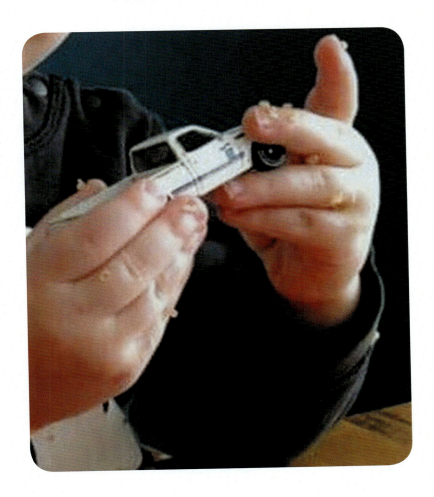

May cause me concern

This little hand

Will learn to share

This little hand

That's one of a pair

This little hand

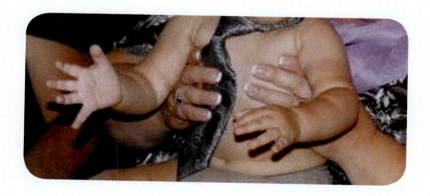

Will know love and praise

This little hand

To which I am so amazed

This little hand

Will do greatness one day

This little hand

Will know God I pray

This little hand

Will have faith that lasts

This little hand

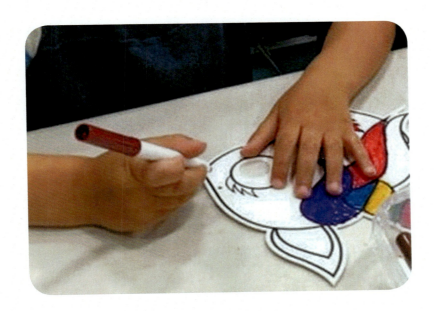

Will not be surpassed

This little hand

Will show kindness I know

This little hand

As pure as the snow

This little hand

Grows so fast

This little hand

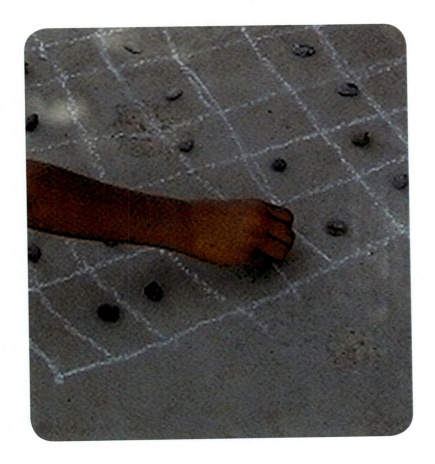

Might be first or last

This little hand

Will have friendships forever

This little hand

Is so very clever

This little hand

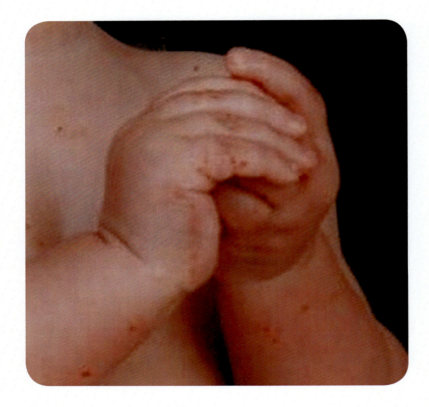

So tiny and small

This little hand

That's hardly at all

Nelda was One of a Kind! She showed her PIZZAZ to the world with her great sense of humor and contagious laughter. She received her College Diploma in Early Childhood Education using it while working at the Cranbrook, B.C. Boys and Girls Club where there was plenty of laughing, playing, singing and storytelling.

Nelda loved working with children, but most of all it was the playing at their level that truly captured her heart.

Printed in the United States
By Bookmasters